AFTER THE

Rain

IS

GONE

Daily Walking with God

Dianne Walker

ISBN: 978-1-960853-42-4

Liberation's Publishing LLC
Columbus - Mississippi

AFTER THE

Rain

IS

GONE

Daily Walking with God

Table of Content

DEDICATION

I dedicate this book to those responsible for my being in existence, My Lord and Savior Jesus Christ, My mother and father, Mr. And Mrs. William King Sr. They keep giving life to my past, present and future.

When I was just a little girl, I remember sitting on the floor in the front doorway of our house. It was raining. I was sad as I sat there watching the rain fall. I wanted to go outside and play. There wasn't much to do as a child growing up in the country, and going outside to play was the best part of the day. We had such a large family, thirteen of us children and then mom and dad. We didn't have much to live off of. We didn't have the luxury of store-bought toys. We definitely didn't' have things to play with inside of the house. We would make toys like houses out of cardboard boxes. We would use mud to form play-food. We played jacks with rocks. These simple handmade toys and activities would keep up excitement all day. Playing house, after the things we saw our parents do, was the most fun. We would rush to finish our chores so we could play whatever activity was on our agenda. The activities all took place outside, but when it rained, we couldn't go outside.

But, Oh Boy! As soon as the rain stopped, outside we would go. Most of the time, after it rained, the sun would come out shining brightly and everything would look clean and smell fresh. We had even more fun. We could play in the mud puddles with our bare feet just enjoying God's creation not even realizing or understanding the beauty God had just made. Sometimes there would be a rainbow in the sky, and we had fun naming the colors as we marveled at it. I can imagine God smiling at our innocence. There was nothing bad in our little world. It was just another day to have more fun.

I have a granddaughter who has been living back and forth between my oldest daughter, her mom, and me her entire life. Her name is Dionna Preshous Joseph. It's hard for me not to favor her, because she is always with me everywhere I go. My friends call her my twin. Some call her my shadow. I had to mention her because of her response to my reading my introduction. She had just turned thirteen. She says to me, "Granny." That's her name for me. "Granny, you don't need to put "Playing house" in there?

"Why not?" I asked.

"It doesn't mean the same thing as it did back then." She replied.

"Okay." I told her.

I know that playing house back then was us imitating our parents. Our parents had rules that we don't have today. Children went outside to play when other adults came over. There were things children were not allowed to see or know. We just played as if we were our parents. Things do change. Nowadays children rarely go outside, because of technology. Parents' teachings are different from what they used to be as well, but that's another book.

In the beginning, I wanted to title the book, "Daily Walking with God" only. But the more I looked at what I wanted to say, my subject changed. Keep in mind that it's a continuation of my first book. Thus, my title, "After the Rain Is Gone" subtitled, "Daily Walking with God." After the rain was gone off of the face of the earth, Noah built an altar unto the Lord and offered burnt offerings on that altar. This was thanksgiving for saving their lives from the waters that fell for forty-day and forty-nights. All the time it was raining Noah, and his family were shut-up inside the ark. This is where I got my subject and how I related my rainy days to the days of Noah and his family being safe from the rain by being shut up inside. My rainy days where the days that I didn't really know God or have a relationship with Him. After my rainy days had passed, I was able to give God praise just as Noah did after the rain was gone. It was time to celebrate the goodness of God.

So many lives were lost in the rain, but God kept Noah and his family safe from the rain. The way God kept me safe during my rainy days and the evils of this world. Everyone didn't make it out of the rain but Praise His Holy Name! He saved me. I was reminded of my life before I had a real relationship with God. I knew of Him but didn't' really know Him. My life was quite different. I cared for the things of the world. So, naturally I was doing my own thing. But God was always there. However, I never really gave Him much thought. I was just existing and doing whatever I knew to do from watching other people who really had no direction themselves. My life had no real meaning. Actually, I was lost just drifting through life. As I said in my first book, I was the four Ps in poverty, parched, in pain, and without purpose. I was searching for what I thought was love, not knowing what I was searching for. Men didn't' have it to give me, only God. He was the only one who could fill the emptiness I felt deep inside. This was when it was raining in my life. I didn't' even know it, but those days I spent shut up on the inside of myself, quiet, not having much to say, was because it was raining in my life. I didn't even know it. Introverted and quiet, afraid of my own shadow. I was fearful of crowds, of people, and, Lord knows, what else I was afraid of.

As I sat and really thought about it, it made sense that I had all of this fear. My mother would always send me to stay with these old people to help them out. One lady was sick and lived in this big old house that was very scary for a little girl like me. I was married at fifteen years old; I was just a child myself and that was scary. I didn't' know how to cook and all of a sudden, I had to figure that out. My husband stood six feet three inches tall, and he was five years older than me. He was the first love of my life.

Then at sixteen my first child was born. He was sick when he was born, then I got sick. We were both in the same hospital at the same time. My husband's sisters were with my baby, and I was alone. The people in the hospital said that my son needed his mother, because his aunts were just little girls themselves. I was still sick, so I had my baby brought to me while I was still recovering in the hospital. That was really terrifying to me. My baby and I were discharged from the hospital, and we went home to my mom's house, so my mother could help me get back up on my feet and help me with the baby. After that I went back to my husband, and we lived with his mother.

I say I don't' know where the fear came from, but I do see it. It would be strange if I wasn't fearful. All of the people, places, and things that I was afraid of took root in my life. Some of my fears were valid. Some weren't so valid, but to a child, who knows the difference. They were all valid. I had no one to lead me through them. What I have learned is to persevere in the face of fear. I know now that God hasn't given us the spirit of fear, but power, love, and a sound mind. Jesus made a world of difference in my life. Things I couldn't manage before, are manageable now through the Spirit of God. What a wonderful blessing to have such loving God in your life who you know loves you and not have to wonder about it. You just know.

EXPOSITION

My rainy days were days filled with fear, hurt, no direction, not knowing what I was doing or how to deal with problems, difficulties, or storms that came with life. The worst fear can be paralyzing. It can stop you from moving forward in life. It is crippling. You feel as if you always have to look over your shoulders. I didn't like crowds of people. I was afraid someone would judge me or talk about me. I was bound by so many different fears. I was locked up on the inside, but no one knew this except God. I didn't understand the fear. I thought it was my genetics. Something tragic happened that caused it. After really thinking about I, it wasn't just one thing but a combination of many things that I went through that placed that fear in me. No one helped me through my fear or explained what was happening to me or why.

Being placed in adult situations as a child was the biggest contributor. As a child it was hard to put things together or make sense of the events in my life. Now I know that God hadn't given me the fear. He gave me power, love, and a sound mind. I know that now. 2 Timothy 1:7, ***"For God has not given us a spirit of fear, but of power and of love and of a sound mind."***

Just in writing this book I am forced to look back over my childhood traumas and remember them, it's clear where my fear came from. This fear came to stop me from purpose. It's a terrible way to live, always in fear of one thing or another. I was always worrying about what people thought of me and fearful of what they may say. Seeds had definitely been planted at an early age that grew bigger and bigger. But God! But God! Say it one more time, but God delivered me!

It was one night at a revival held at my home church, Town Creek M.B. Church, I will never forget it. The guest preacher for that revival was a well-known pastor in the area, Pastor Jonathan Tucker from New Albany Ms. Pastor Tucker was preaching this particular night a message named "Breaking Free." One thing he said that night while he was preaching blessed me forever. What he said was, "some of you don't have to break free, because you are already free." He gave an example. He said, "It's like you're sitting in jail, the door is open, and all you have to do is just get up and walk out. God has already freed some of you, but you're still sitting there like you're still bound." Oh my God! That word sat in my spirit, and that night I walked out.

Hallelujah! Praise God's holy name! I realized that I was already free from so many things, and all I had to do was to walk in the victory of God. He had freed me, and his blood, and the words of my testimony keeps me free. Revelation 12:11 **And they overcame him by the blood of the Lamb and by the word of their testimony, and they did not love their lives to the death.**

Being saved and keeping a good relationship with God helps to keep us free from all fears. Another way to say it is, "Daily walking with God." In walking with God, we learn how to walk above the natural and carnal world. It's not where you find God. God is a spirit, and they that worship him must worship Him in Spirit and Truth for the Father seeketh such to worship Him. Don't get me wrong, God is always with His children. It's just in order to fellowship with Him, we must be in the Spirit. He said in Matthew 28:20, **"I am with you always even unto the end of the world."**

When you walk above the natural world, it doesn't mean you are no longer human. We aren't just human we are spirits also. We learn to walk in the spirit In order to walk with God. We can't make it in this life without God. We need to daily walk with Him. When your relationship with God is such that, you are close enough to Him to walk with Him then you can have fellowship with Him. God is not just with us for no reason. He is there to walk alongside us, aid us, and help us. He is our helper. He makes our ministry effectual for the discipline of the nations, for the pulling down of strongholds of Satan, and the setting up of God's kingdom for the Lord Jesus.

The Meaning of Walking with God

When we walk with God it may not make things easier. It does make them possible. Walking with Him gives us assurance of His presence and power in our lives. We can overcome because our God is all powerful and with Him all things are possible. We can endure trial, heartache, and whatever life throws our way. Because of His resurrection power in us, we are overcomers. We know these things are true. Amen!

HOW TO WALK WITH GOD DAILY!

Walking with God is a step-by-step process. You must be in the Spirit and in His will. Our lives must be in line with God's word. We can't come to a Holy god any kind of way. We must be clean by the washing of the word. Hence the need to read the word daily. You can take a verse and think about it, meditate on it. Seek out the meaning of it, and what it means to you and your life. Read as much as you are led to read. The point of it all is to spend time in the Word. Just like exercise, to see results you must remain faithful to it in order to see the results you want. Do the necessary things, read, study to grow in Christ. Walking with God also means talking to Him. We talk to God in prayer. We just don't do all of the talking; we are waiting for answers and clarity. God may have something He wants to say to you as well. Prayer is a dialog. So, sit silently for a while and listen to Him.

The dialog will not be how we talk to each other. He speaks to our hearts. Many times, a verse of Scripture will come to mind. So, think about it. You will understand what He is saying to you. This is how He communicates to us today, through His word. The bible teaches us that we must pray without ceasing. In Hebrews 4:16 it says, **"Let us therefore come boldly to the throne of grace, that we may obtain mercy and find grace** to help in time of need." Then Hebrews 1:1-2 says, "**God, who at sundry times and in divers manners spake in time past unto the fathers by the prophets, Hath in these last days spoken unto us by his Son, whom he hath appointed heir of all things, by whom also he made the worlds;**" (KJV)

This is how we talk to God, through prayer. We must prepare our hearts and mind to commune with an almighty God. We must read and study His word. Then we must talk to Him in prayer. These are steps we take in a daily walk with God. Genesis 5:24 says, **"And Enoch walked with God: and he was not; for God took him."** The word walk in the bible is a biblical expression for obedience and fellowship with God. The result of it is divine favor. It refers to the manner of life a person lives close to God. Enoch walked with God. His walk was a walk of dedication, devotion, and closeness. His walk lived up to his name. Enoch means Dedicated. To walk with God also means that you and God agree about your life. In Amos 3:3 it says, **"Can two walk together, except they be agreed?"**

NOAH'S WALK

Noah also walked with God. In Genesis 6:9 it says, **"These are the generations of Noah: Noah was a just man and perfect in his generations, and Noah walked with God."** Imagine being Noah and hearing God's command to build an ark. Noah was around five-hundred years old at this time. He had walked faithfully with God and wasn't about to stop. The ark would have been massive; the work and task huge. In spite of it all Noah obeyed God and went to work. In Noah's day the people on earth were corrupt and unwilling to join Noah on his walk of obedience. They laughed and made fun of the work he was doing. Noah persevered and built the ark that would save him and his family. Not only did the ark save Noah's family but all of the animals and other creations of God.

Walking with God may mean looking foolish to others while staying true to God. A true and real walk with God means fellowship with Him, praying seriously and listening to what God has to say to you, and following His directions. 1 Samuel 3:9 says, **"Speak, Lord, for your servant is listening!"** It means acting on divine wisdom that will seem like foolishness in the mind of a godless world. 1 Corinthians 1:18-31 says,

18 For the preaching of the cross is to them that perish foolishness; but unto us which are saved it is the power of God. 19 For it is written, I will destroy the wisdom of the wise and will bring to nothing the understanding of the prudent. 20 Where is the wise? Where is the scribe? Where is the disputer of this world? hath not God made foolish the

wisdom of this world?

21 For after that in the wisdom of God the world by wisdom knew not God, it pleased God by the foolishness of preaching to save them that believe. 22 For the Jews require a sign, and the Greeks seek after wisdom: 23 But we preach Christ crucified, unto the Jews a stumbling block, and unto the Greeks foolishness; 24 But unto them which are called, both Jews and Greeks, Christ the power of God, and the wisdom of God. 25 Because the foolishness of God is wiser than men; and the weakness of God is stronger than men.

26 For ye see your calling, brethren, how that not many wise men after the flesh, not many mighty, not many noble, are called: 27 But God hath chosen the foolish things of the world to confound the wise; and God hath chosen the weak things of the world to confound the things which are mighty; 28 And base things of the world, and things which are despised, hath God chosen, yea, and things which are not, to bring to nought things that are: 29 That no flesh should glory in his presence. 30 But of him are ye in Christ Jesus, who of God is made unto us wisdom, and righteousness, and sanctification, and redemption: 31 That, according as it is written, He that glorieth, let him glory in the Lord."

Was Noah perfect? Hardly. Noah stumbled later in his walk when he became drunk and subjected himself to ridicule. Genesis 9:20-23 reads, **"20 And Noah began to be a husbandman, and he planted a vineyard: 21 And he drank of the wine and was drunken; and he was uncovered within his tent. 22 And Ham, the father of Canaan, saw the nakedness of his father, and told his two brethren without.**

23 And Shem and Japheth took a garment, and laid it upon both their shoulders, and went backward, and covered the nakedness of their father; and their faces were backward, and they saw not their father's nakedness."

We don't have to be perfect to be used by God in remarkable ways. God used Noah to make a new start with the human race. What will He do with you?

THE WOMAN AT THE WELL'S WALK

Readying Your Heart

Now walk with me as we go on this journey walking with God, form deliverance to service. John 4:25 says, "**The woman saith unto him, I know that Messias cometh, which is called Christ: when he is come, he will tell us all things.**" Let me just say this, Christ will show Himself to those who with an honest and humble heart desire to be acquainted with Him. In John 4:25 the woman at the well was prepared to receive such a relationship, because she had great expectation of the Messiah and was ready to receive instructions from Him. It is not written in the text whether she had an opportunity to see Christ miracles which was the ordinary method of conviction, in those days, to see and believe. God has secret ways of making sure His people get what they need; and she was prepared to receive her "Better." Better than she had already experienced, and whatever God had in store for her, she was open to receive.

For most people that have no sense of purpose there comes a time in their life that they ready themselves to receive it. When they just get tired of the stupid stuff and start looking for the real meaning of why we are here. God didn't make us for us to wonder aimlessly through life, but to be in fellowship with Him, so that we can accomplish the purpose He has set for His people. We are not waiting on God, God is waiting on us to ready ourselves to receive Him wholehearted, ready to put Him first and to leave the things of this world behind so that we can have that abundant life He promised. After the woman at the well realized, she was talking to the Messiah, she was ready, open, and expecting a better life. He blessed her with living water, water that never runs out. It was water that once consumed would overflow into everlasting life. She was ready to begin her service for the Lord.

He didn't have to tell her to go and do this or that. She immediately dropped her water pot, went into the city, and told the men, "Come see a Man that told me everything that I ever did." Yes, she went to those who she was familiar with, men. They may have been some of the same men she had serviced. They would probably been some of the first to cast a stone at her. It's funny how God will allow you to go back to the same people who were in the same mess as you. That's the problem with a lot of us today, we don't want to let go of our pots. Whatever they may be, we like what we are doing and love what we are getting, so we think because we really don't know or understand. It is kind of like Asap. In Psalm 73:2-3 in the bible whose foot almost slipped when he saw the prosperity of the wicked. In Hebrews 12:1 it says, **"wherefore seeing we also are compassed about with so great a cloud of witnesses, let us lay aside every weight, and the sin which doth so easily beset us, and let us run with patience the race that is set before us."**

Jesus is the way, truth, and the light, all of us must come to Him by way of the cross, in this process or order. There were steps that had to take place in order for the woman at the well's condition to change. It started with a conversation with Jesus. Out of the conversation came conviction, and then confession and lastly a changed condition. What Jesus said thus far concerning His grace and eternal life had made little if any impression upon her, because she had not yet been convinced of her sins. He moves from the conversation about living water and sets Himself to awaken her conscious, to open the wounds of guilt. She would be able to apprehend the remedy more easily, by grace, or in other words receive the cure for her condition. How discreetly and decently Christ introduces this conversation. How industriously the woman seeks to evade the conviction, and yet insensibly convicts herself, and before she's aware, admits her faults. "I have no husband." She confesses. How closely our Lord Jesus, brings home the conviction to her conscious. It's probable that He said more than is recorded, because she said that He told her all she ever did. Jesus leaves it to her own conscious to say the rest.

Reproofs are ordinarily most profitable when they are least provoking, not mean, or harsh speaking, but with love and compassion, as someone with real concern. I talked in my first book of the method that Jesus used to bring people to Himself, which was the love method. Sin has a way of blinding its victims to their sins, and love is just the opposite. It draws them out of the darkness and bring them into God's marvelous light.

Even though Jesus had to bring this woman to conviction, He did it in a loving way. It's not always what you say but how you say it. As children of God, it's our duty to bring people to Christ, not to drive them away. Many of God's people are harsh with their words, and words can hurt, even wound a person for life. So many of us lack compassion and are very careless with our words. This makes them ineffective in helping people find their way to Christ. As children of God, we should have the fruit of the spirit. I know it may take time to take on all the traits of the spirit, but we should be working on it daily, taking off all things that are not of God. The Holy Spirit will equip us with this fruit if we allow Him. I have seen some really mean Christians that hide who they really are to the world. It's not a pretty picture. God's way is a great way to bring people to Christ. Who should know better than the Lord Himself, Our awesome God!

MY WALK WITH GOD

Wherefore seeing we also are compassed about with so great a cloud of witnesses, let us lay aside every weight, and the sin which doth so easily beset us, and let us run with patience the race that is set before us.

When we lay aside our weights and sins then we can follow God fervently! Anything that hinders or hold us back from giving God our all is either weight or sin and needs to be laid aside. When we are ready, He will be there for us. I remember preparing my heart to receive God like it was yesterday. God had already changed my life. He set me free and gave my life real meaning. There wasn't one thing that brought me to this point. There was a combination of many things. One thing I know is I was simply tired of my life the way it was. I wanted better. I suddenly had the desire to read my bible and to start spending time with the Lord. I knew there was more to life than what I had experienced, and I was searching for it.

Each day after my children were off to school I sat down with my bible. I had no idea where I would start reading, but one day I ended up in first and second Corinthians. I continued to read those two books all week. These two books focused was unity, and that the followers of Jesus are held to a standard of integrity and morality. We seek to represent His new way of life to our communities and encourage believers to embrace and follow the way of Jesus. This way transforms our lives and values, generosity, humility, and weakness. These were things I was struggling with and what I needed. After reading and studying God's word all that week my heart was ready to obey. God knew I was ready and real, in what I was asking Him for.

Leading up to the Sunday that my life changed forever, I spent that Saturday in prayer talking with God. One of the things that I prayed and promised was that I was going to clean up my outside and I wanted Him to clean up my inside. That Sunday I dressed in modest attire, no make-up, and no jewelry. This was my way of cleaning up my outside, not knowing God was already working on my inside as I prayed and studied His word. As I sat there reading, tears rolled down my face. He was working on my inside through His word. I just didn't know or understand what was happening to me. When I made it to church that Sunday morning, it dawned on me that it was my physical birth month, which is September. I am in church sitting on the pew as the Pastor preached. The Pastor was also my blood brother Pastor Jessie King Sr. I sat there thinking and waiting on God to do what I had asked Him to do. Now, I didn't know what that entailed. Pastor King finished his message and extended the invitation to salvation. He said, "if anyone here wants to be saved, you can come."

I sat there reasoning with myself. I thought, "you're already saved." So, I didn't move. He asked again and added, "Someone here today just wants to be closer to God." This made me come to the edge of my seat. "Okay that's me." I thought. I got up from my seat and headed down the aisle. When I reached the altar, that was the last time I would remember my natural self. It was as if I left my body. I was no longer in control. It was as if I was taken to another place. All I could sense was love, peace, joy and so much light, bright light, in my subconscious. I knew I was in the presence of the Lord, and it seemed as if time stood still. I am sure it was only a few minutes, but for me it seemed like a long time. I had a sense of being safe and loved that I had never experienced before. I felt new and elevated. God had changed my heart and made me over. I had been filled with His precious Spirit. I didn't really know what I had been asking for all of this time. This was way more than I had expected.

When I came back to myself it was me but not me. I was different, changed, made over. God had done exactly what I had asked Him to do for me. What a mighty God we serve! He has done unto me a great and mighty thing. From that brief encounter with God, I would never be the same, nor did I want to be. God changed even my "want to Be's." Hallelujah! Praise His most holy name. I left church that Sunday, a new person. I didn't leave the same way I went. I don't think the people there knew or understood what had happened to me. The pastor knew because later when we talked, he said something was different about me. I had a glow. He had had a similar experience.

I had been elevated, as if I was walking on clouds. I was singing divine songs that I had never heard before. My spirit was singing. Today I couldn't reproduce them or tell you how they sounded. I couldn't sleep from praising Him. I even praised him in my sleep. Everyone I came into contact with I shared the good news of the gospel. I couldn't help myself. He was all over me. I just couldn't stop talking and telling people about His goodness. I was on the phone calling people that I knew, friends and family. When I tell you, I know how the woman at the well felt when she dropped her water pot and ran into the city crying, "come see a man!" I forgot about my old life. Whatever I had been doing before this didn't even come up. I had only one thing on my mind, and that was to get as many people to Christ as I could. "Come see a man who told me all that I had I ever done."

I started my walk with God so happy and filled with joy and praise for Him. I don't know how many weeks, or months. It seemed like there was no time limit. I wasn't watching or counting time, so I don't know how much time had passed with me feeling like this and walking in closeness with God. That is until the man that I was in love with showed back up into my life again.

Of course, Satan wouldn't have it any other way. I am sure he took Council with his cohorts to put an end to all this spreading of the good news of God's word, and the singing of His praises, all the praise of His holy name. So, the fact that he would show up now, right after my encounter with God was no surprise or coincidence. Mind you at this time it didn't register with me that this was a test. It was later on that I came to realize that it was to hurt God.

Now I know you are sitting on the edge of your seat to find out what happened, because I can hardly contain myself. I'll try to explain it as clearly as I possibly can. I will try to paint a picture for you. This was not one of my husbands. Just as Jesus said to the woman at the well, "the one you are with now is not your husband." Now this was that one. The one I really loved and had passion for. When he showed up in town it was on and popping, that one. Now even though the wonderful thing God had done were fresh, and my life had changed and to that there is no doubt, my flesh went into overdrive. After all I loved this man, and my flesh craved his touch. I tried to fight my feelings by giving him a detailed explanation of what just happened to me, in the hopes that he would just respect me enough to not pursue intimate time with me. I didn't want to fall back into my old ways. He could just leave if he had to. I was hoping he would help me to say no, do things the right way if we wanted to be together. We needed to do it God's way. Unfortunately, that was not the case.

I fell, and great was the fall. I let God down, after all He had just done for me. This was my time to shine. I had everything I needed to stand. It was not like it was before God blessed me; it was after. I was equipped with the power to say no but let my flesh get the better of me. I chose to go back. I went back to Egypt, back to bondage. I did it because I remembered the links and melons, how good they were. I forgot about all the bad times when I had to make bricks without straw. Now you have to go and read the story of the children of Israel's exodus from Egypt if you don't understand what I am talking about. It was not that I couldn't help myself, it was my choice. To this day I don't understand how I allowed my flesh to erase all God had done for me in a few seconds. No one had ever been that good to me. I lost myself in my own desires. God was no longer first. I put myself in first place, which is a grave sin. I became my god, or better yet, I allowed him to become my God. Either way anyone or anything we put before God, becomes our god.

1 Corinthians 10:13, "**There hath no temptation taken you, but such as is common to man: but God is faithful, who will not suffer you to be tempted above that ye are able; but will with the temptation also make a way to escape, that ye may be able to bear it.**"

There was no flaw in what God had done for me. The flaws were in me. I had a lot more growing to do. God knew I would fall even before I fell, and He still blessed me because He loved me that much. God looked at the overall picture, the finished product. It's not that I was going to be this huge great life changer, or maybe I would be, God knows. He looked at my heart. He knew that I wanted to be the best I could be for Him. I want Him to be proud of me, for what I would accomplish in His name. Yes, I had fallen. After the lust and passion were gone God still loved me. Yes, I say lust because real love would have waited till it was right on both sides. We would've done it God's way and not our own way. There are consequences for our sins. My newness was gone. My freshness was gone. My excitement was gone, and my elevation was brought low. I lost my joy, but God never deserted me. He was still right there with me.

Satan on the other hand, had accomplished his mission. He had gained this victory, won this battle, but little did he know he hadn't won the war. I was more determined than ever to make it right with God and get back on track. The man that I was so in love with apologized, because he could feel that something was different this time. He was sorry that he had played a part in Satan's plan to bring me down. He left and I was left alone with my thoughts, shame, and hurt. I had hurt God and let Him down. I found myself on my face before Him begging for forgiveness, and He forgave me.

This was the first fall after God had made me new, but it wasn't my last. Getting back on track with God, I gathered myself with the help of the Holy Spirit, and I continued my walk with the Lord. A large lesson I learn early in my walk with the Lord is that it's a daily walk, one day at a time. A day's toil is enough for us to attend to if we are walking with God. In His will and His ways, a day at a time is enough.

Getting Back on Track

Matthew 6:34, "**Take therefore no thought for the morrow: for the morrow shall take thought for the things of itself. Sufficient unto the day is the evil thereof**." Getting back on track with God, really means getting back to basics. Sin separates us from God, so we must confess, repent, and turn from sin in order to get our closeness back with God. We do that through prayer. We talk to God and pour out our heart to Him and let Him know that we are sorry and don't want to do that sin anymore. Spend alone time with God, in His word. Studying the things that will help us grow, to do better and not go backwards. That is a trick from the enemy to keep you looking backwards.

It took some time for me to get my joy back, because God had forgiven me, but I hadn't forgiven myself. How could I have given in to my flesh? It replayed in my mind over and over as I grieved the loss of my new and wonderful relationship with The Lord. The Lord allowed me to wallow in my grief for a while. Satan dragged me through mistakes. I kept asking myself questions like, what was wrong with me? God had done a great thing for me. He had cleaned me up, and I repaid Him by getting dirty all over again. After being set free, I look back in Proverbs 26:11, where it says, "**as a dog return to his vomit, so a fool repeats his folly.**"

It's just that bad. I felt every bit of it. I had no excuse with all of the help God had deposited on the inside of me. The voice kept screaming at me. I finally silenced the voice by giving my flesh what it wanted and ignoring my Spirit. Guilt is not of God. It is straight from the devil, and he is the ultimate condemner. He keeps you feeling bad, so you can't help anyone else. How can you help someone else when you are feeling condemned yourself? Now that's a trick of the devil. You just have to remember what was said in the book of Micah 7:18-19 **"Who is a God like unto thee, that pardoneth iniquity, and passeth by the transgression of the remnant of his heritage? He retaineth not his anger forever, because he delighteth in mercy. 19 He will turn again; he will have compassion upon us; he will subdue our iniquities; and thou wilt cast all their sins into the depths of the sea."**

God doesn't remember our sins. He did this for our sins, past, present, and future. He took it upon himself for us and that is it. It is finished. A debt paid in full that we no longer owe. We are made free by our belief in Him as Lord, and Savior. We don't have to allow Satan to make us feel bad if we fall, because we are not running into sin. We are running from sin and sometimes we trip and fall. We don't live in sin. We live in our life after Christ. The way He wants us to live. The Holy Spirit is forever with us helping us to live a Godly life. All we need to do is lean and depend on Him.

THE CONVERSATION

A conversation is a talk between two or more people, in which news and ideas are exchanged. This is what was going on between Jesus and the Samaritan woman at the well. This conversation started when Jesus asked this woman for a drink of water. This woman being a Samaritan was shocked, because she could see that Jesus was a Jew and knew that the Jews had no dealings with the Samaritans. However, Jesus never entertained what the woman said concerning the conflict between the two. He gets right to the point of His mission, why He was really there. He said, "if you knew the gift of God and who it is that said to you, give me to drink, you would have asked of Him, and He would have given you living water." Now with that Jesus sparked her curiosity. She obviously wanted to know more about this living water. This conversation was orchestrated by Jesus to draw her in, and that it did.

I guess the woman thinking things over, in return asked Jesus, "why would I ask you for a drink? You don't even have anything to draw with and the well is deep, so where are you going to get this living water, you are talking about?" She wants to know more of what Jesus is talking about. She can only think of what she knows, the natural things. She is wondering, "hold up, are you greater than our father Jacob who gave us this well and used it for himself and his family?" Jesus goes past all of this and gets to the point of the conversation. He tells her whoever drinks this water that I give shall never thirst again and that water will be in him, a well of water springing up into everlasting life. Now after hearing about this water and what it does, she asks for this water, so she wouldn't have to come and draw or be thirsty again.

She doesn't know that Jesus was preparing her to receive this living water all the while. He tells her to go call her husband. It's at this time in the conversation that the Samaritan woman is convicted. In her conversation with Jesus, she tells Him she has no husband. Jesus tells her she had said right. She had no husband. She has had five husbands and the one she now has is not hers. I can't really say what Jesus meant in the statement, "the one you have now is not yours." He could have been saying she was just living with him, and they weren't married. He could have been married to someone else, but in any case, he wasn't hers and wasn't married to her. This was clear. It was obvious she was confronted by Jesus about her sins and convicted by her own conscience. This leaves her with nothing else to do but confess. This is just what she did.

When she said I have no husband, the conviction and confession brought about a change in her. When we are truly repentant, we are forgiven for our sins. We are freed from guilt and shame. As long as we stay in our sins, we have no fellowship with God. We must confess and forsake our sins. This woman does not deny the truth of what Jesus charged her with. She owned her charges of reproof from the LORD. She speaks respectfully to Him, calls Him Sir, and acknowledges Him to be a Prophet, one that had some correspondence with heaven.

The conversation is part of what Jesus used to bring about

a change in this woman's life. Pay close attention as you read this section. Don't miss the process Jesus is using in this text to bring her to Christ. Romans 10:17 says, **"So then faith cometh by hearing, and hearing by the word of God."** We begin to have faith and strength by hearing the word of God. God gives faith, but it is by the word. The word is the instrument in which we believe. We must have first heard.

As Jesus speaks to the woman at the well. His words sank deep into her soul to a place that she thought no one could reach, a place of brokenness and hurt. This was the set of her wounding that caused faith to rise up in her from the depths of despair came hope. Jesus being no ordinary man, and his words have power, power to change lives. There is life in God's words. When we honestly sit down with God's word and in honesty want to know Him, His will, and His ways. The word will honestly come alive in our hands and heart. How do I know? I have experienced it. So, after having this conversation with Jesus, this woman was not the same. Her whole life changed, and it changed for the better. So, we need to hear the spoken word which is call the "Rhema" or preached word and the written word. The Bible is called the Logos. We need both to hear and study the word of God. This woman was in a conversation face to face with Jesus. However, we can't have face to face conversation with God. We can have conversation with God through prayer.

He encourages us to pray without ceasing, which means He enjoys having conversations with us. There is nothing too big or too small that we can't talk to God about it. There is no time or place that we can't talk to Him all through the day as we work, as we minster to others. We use our gifts just sitting at home, walking down the street shopping. He is always listening. His ears are always open to what we have to say. Now isn't that a blessing all by itself? To have a God who cares so much about us. Praise His Holy Name! 1Thessalonians 5:17, "Pray without ceasing."

Her Condition Changed

The woman at the well had a condition. She was lost. After her conversation with Jesus her condition changed again. She went from being lost to being saved. The condition of a person is the state of the person. If a person has not accepted Jesus as their Lord and Savior, they are in a state of being lost. Those that believe are in a saved state. How does a person go from lost to saved? I'm so glad you asked. In order to be saved a person must have faith in our Lord and Savior Jesus Christ. The book of Romans 10:9-10 says, **"That if thou shalt confess with thy mouth the Lord Jesus, and shalt believe in thine heart that God hath raised him from the dead, thou shalt be saved. For with the heart man believeth unto righteousness; and with the mouth confession is made unto salvation."**

In order to live in a saved state, one's condition must change from lost to found. This is done by confession. You must believe with your mind and in your heart. With the heart man believes that Jesus was born into the world of a virgin birth by the Holy Spirit. He lived here thirty-three-and-one-half years and died on the cross for our sins. He was buried in a borrowed tomb and three days later he rose from death. We must believe this in our hearts and confess from our mouths, and our condition will change.

When the woman at the well believed in Jesus as Lord she

was saved, and her condition changed. Everything in her life changed as it did for me. It is that way for any who have had a true encounter with God. I can only speak of what is written and what the Holy Spirit has given me from the story of the woman at the well. The story is broad. It may fit anyone who needs it. It speaks of the heart of people. If you really want to walk with God, you must be willing to give yourself to Him completely. It is a total surrender to the Lord.

Many have been broken and hurt and need a savior. If you really want to walk with God, you must be willing to give yourself to him. Many get saved and leave it there. That is as far as they go. They never get to know God in an intimate way. They never allow God to fill them, because they don't want to separate from the things of the world. They feel they won't have fun. That is because they have not experienced the fun in a total surrender to God. Satan would have you believe that serving God is boring and all the good times are over. That is one of the biggest lies ever told. He wants to keep you living a worldly life and remain a friend of the world and an enemy with God. James 4:4 says, **"Ye adulterers and adulteresses, know ye not that the friendship of the world is enmity with God? whosoever therefore will be a friend of the world is the enemy of God."**

I can talk in detail about my story because I know my story. As for the woman at the well her information is limited. This lets me know that people are not so forgiving or loving. We must be led by the Holy Spirit on what information to share with others. This woman was now a new person. She started out a specimen of impurity and now a teacher of evangelical truth. Her condition changed which changed everything in her life, as it does with everyone who has a real encounter with

God. I found my story in her story, and it helped me through my pain, hurt, and brokenness. In my first book I shared what I called Jesus' course of spiritual physics.

This is simply Jesus's way of bringing people to Himself. He does this by simply opening the wound of guilt so that an individual can easily comprehend the remedy of God's grace. This is the same method that Jesus used with the woman at the well. After being made weary and heavy laden under the burden of sin and brought to Christ for rest. I was moved in the Spirit to give a little more information on this process that Jesus used. In case someone is reading this book that condition is lost. You have not accepted Jesus as Lord. This means the belief that a virgin named Mary conceived Jesus by the Holy Ghost and gave birth to Him. He lived here on earth for thirty-three and a half years teaching and preaching, healing the sick, casting out demons, raising the dead, and many other miracles. He finished it all by going to the cross and giving his life so that we may live.

So, then we put our trust in Him for our salvation. We believe in our hearts and confess with our mouth that we believe all the words I've spoken. When we are saved our condition changes from lost to saved. To God be the glory! When a person is lost, they don't have the Holy Spirit living inside of them to help them live a holy life, life according to the way God wants us to live. The Holy Spirit helps us in time to take on the fruit of the spirit which are love, joy, peace, patience, kindness, goodness, faithfulness, gentleness, and self-control. Without the Holy Spirit a person rarely possesses these traits. We need the Holy Spirit to help us become what God wants us to be. This is why Jesus called Him our helper. Some of us would never come to repentance if it was not for someone confronting us about our sins. It's possible that King David would have never pinned the fifty-first, Psalm, had he not been confronted by the prophet Nathan for his sins, of taking another man's wife and having him killed. The bible speaks of King David as a man after God's own heart.

This was what Jesus used, the subject of water, to discuss one of the greatest truths of spiritual life, that of living water. To the Jews' living water was water that was always flowing and moving along, such as a creek fed by springs or a like with an inflow and an outflow. Dead water was stagnant water, such as ponds or pools that were always sitting still with no inflow or outflow. However, when Jesus spoke of living water, He meant much more than living streams and lakes. This living water is of God. It is of Him who is living, always has, and always will be living. The water that God gives is the most alive water there is. No other water, no matter how alive it may be considered, can compare with the living water that is God. It's always overflowing into everlasting life.

John 3:16 says, **"God so loved the world that he gave his only begotten Son, that whosoever believe in him shall not perish but have everlasting life."** God made man in a perfect state, but man fell from grace, in other words disobeyed God, which was sin, and his fall caused sin to fall on all mankind. We all were in Adam's loins for lack of a better word. His decedents. So, because God loved us so that in the book of Hebrews 10:5 it says, **"wherefore when he cometh into the world, he saith, Sacrifice and offering thou wouldest not but a body hast thou prepared me."**

God prepared Him a body and came to earth to save man Himself. He loved us that much and the least we could do is love and live for Him. We serve an awesome God, Amen.

Hebrews 10:7, **"Then said I, Lo I come in the volume of the book it is written of me to do they will, O'God."** The story of our Lord and Savior Jesus Christ, his mission, how he carried it out, and then ascended back into heaven at the right hand of the Father. Making intersessions still for us. What a mighty God we serve.

Here Interest Changed

This was a dramatic picture of conversion and witnessing. The Messiah was discovered, and the discovery was excitedly shared. This woman had been brought to the knowledge of Christ. She wasn't interested anymore in drawing water because she had water they knew not of. She had something much better. Those who are brought into the knowledge of Christ will show it by a holy contempt of this world. Those who are newly acquainted with the things of God must be excused. If at first, they are so taken up with the new world they have been brought into, that the things of this world seem to be for a time wholly neglected, the world for spiritual. This woman was opened to know and learn. Her belief was the Messiah was coming and would be in authority, but her belief was not a saving belief or a belief of commitment. At this point it was only a mental or intellectual belief. However, she did not reject the witness of Jesus. She was not rude. She listened to him. Therefore, God was able to give her a sense of His presence. The person who constantly rejects Jesus Christ or claims to be agnostic or atheistic is seldom reached for Christ. However, a person wo listens to the Scripture and believes intellectual belief is more open. It is exposed to God's word.

Thereby it is more likely to become a saving belief. The

belief of commitment. Warning: However, a warning does need to be issued. A person with only a mental belief can hear and reject so much that he or she becomes gospel hardened. That is so hardened against the gospel that they never trust Jesus Christ as Savior. My pastor Dr. Charles Davidson of the Town Creek MB church said it best. He said once while preaching that some people are going to miss heaven by eighteen inches which is the distance from our head to our heart. It's with the heart man believes unto righteousness. Truth be told sometimes we know too much, or we are too full to learn anything new. We need to empty ourselves and let God fill us up with what He wants us to know and have, Amen.

Romans 10:10 says, **"For with the heart man believeth unto righteousness and with the mouth confession is made unto salvation."** In chapter four and verse twenty-eight of the gospel of John this woman left her water pot and went into the city. The water pot was for her to draw water, but now she is no longer concerned about drawing water. She goes into the city because now she is interested and caught up in telling the good news that she just heard. She was extremely excited as someone with a burning on the inside. For sure this is new because she is now a new person in Christ Jesus.

2 Corinthians 5:17 says, **"Therefor if any man be in Christ, he is a new creature, and old things are passed away: behold all things are become new."** This woman is now interested in men, but in a different way. Her old interests were for her own benefit and gratification, deeds of the flesh. Her knowing who Jesus is has changed everything in her life. She has a new interest. Now she has a purpose. She has a real reason for being alive, sure enough real reason that means something. A whole new world is opening up to her, and she is

not selfish. She wants to share her new experience with others. How do you explain a real encounter with God? It's not an easy thing to do, for the simple reason that there is no way for the natural to explain the spiritual without sounding foolish to the carnal man. The truth is the carnal mind cannot perceive the things of the spirit. This is so different from anything this woman had ever experienced to have a real encounter with an almighty God means you will never be the same again. Your life changes for the better. It's so good knowing God and having a relationship with Him. It's just awesome. You really don't' want to look back or feel bad about leaving the old life behind. Being so caught up with her new life in Christ.

The woman at the well is ready to start her new life and waste no time. She drops the pot and is off to the city. "Come see a man!" Yes! You move from a life of sin with the weight of life on your shoulders to a life covered by the King of Kings. Wow! From a mind of me, myself, and I to a mind of really caring about other people. You move from where there was envy, jealousy, hate, selfishness, greed, lust, anger, sadness, loneliness, depression, emptiness, to a life of love, joy, peace, happiness, caring for others giving, and being mild tempered. What a change of interest you exchange the old for the new. The old doesn't compare to the new because the new stops. It just keeps bubbling up and bubbling over into everlasting life. There is something that has me puzzled. What is it when a person says they are saved? Their interest doesn't change. They are saved. They were interested in drinking, gambling, partying, cheating on their wives and husbands. They are mean and did things that really hurt people. They were saved and nothing changed. Their profession they still do all the same things they did before they said they were saved.

The idea is to be a new creation in Christ Jesus, and old things pass away. What is going on? I bring this up not to try and burst anyone out or make anyone feel bad. I am sounding an alarm. A lot of people really think they are on their way to heaven but are headed straight to hell. The bible plainly states that no fornicators, neither idol worshippers, adulterers, whoremongers, shall inherit God's kingdom. That's only to mention some of the things I see. There are many other things that people don't allow, old things that people don't want to let go of. Hear me people when I tell you that you will have to stand before a holy God one day and give an account of the deeds done in your body.

Some people believe all they have to do is show up for church on Sunday, and then they can go and do whatever they want to until the next church service. That is the extent of their relationship with God. They have done what they have been taught, no matter how many times they hear the pastor or anyone else say that just coming to church doesn't save you. There must be a changed heart and a changed life. This has been inbred into them, and they see the people that told them these things seem to be doing okay. They like doing what they are doing anyway. They choose to believe a lie. Really what they know is not true. There are two sides to every story. You can have a life with the Lord or a life without the Lord. I guarantee they will look quite different.

The woman at the well had a quite different life before her encounter with Christ. It appears that her interest before encountering Jesus was men and her own gratification. What she wanted after her encounter was new. She no longer cared about the things of her old life. She dropped everything right away and started a new walk with the Lord. So, did I. I am sure that her life was not perfect, and neither was mine. Better. Different. Now because walking with the Lord is better sometimes up, sometimes down. But always walking with God. A new life. A new walk and a new relationship with God. O taste and see that the Lord is good; blessed is the man that trust in Him. I want people to understand, so we stop judging people because some people get saved and never grow in Christ. They never mature. Their lie continues to look like the life of an unbeliever. This is why we can't judge people. Only God knows if someone truly excepted Him in their heart. My warning is to each individual that we know for ourselves that we are saved.

God has given us the assurance that we are saved. One thing I know is it's hard to remain the same when God has his hands on your life. Make sure you don't have any trouble at the river of Jordan, and Jesus will be there to help you to cross. That's a song called, "Jordan River" all that song is saying is don't wait till time to cross over and you still aren't sure if you're really saved. My husband, Pastor Steven Walker always says, "It's better to have God and not need Him, than to need Him and not have him." Let us all just make sure that we have God on our side. Know for yourself that you are saved without any doubt in your heart and mind. Don't be ashamed of getting help if you aren't sure. There was a time when I wasn't sure. I prayed to God and asked Him to clean me up and he did. He gave me the assurance that I was saved. This woman interest changed as did mine. I can't speak for anyone else; I just know for myself.

The woman at the well left her waterpot. Her water pot was a symbol of her old life. It needed to be left behind. When God sends his Holy Spirit into our hearts house cleaning begins.

There are things that need to be cleaned out and the Holy Spirit wastes no time starting the process of cleaning. The Holy Spirit is Holy and therefore desires us to be holy also. He starts to get rid of the things of the old life to replace them with the new. Some friends must be left behind. Some families must be left behind. Some relationships must be left behind, attitudes and actions. Some of our habits will change and our conversations. Her entire behavior changed from worldly to spiritual. Her actions proved that a change had taken place.

She now finds herself in the city witnessing to people about Jesus. There should be a visible change in the life of the believer. It's not about talk, there should be evidence. If there is no change, I think there is something wrong with that picture. I don't believe that you can have a real encounter with the almighty God and stay the same. Not the God I serve anyway. My interests, actions, and life totally changed for the better. Now of course the Holy Spirit did and is still doing a work in me. Some things change right away, while other things take time. I have a saying that God even changed some of my "want to's." In other words, some of my actions before Christ I don't even want to do anymore in my life. Don't get me wrong, all people do wrong, but the difference is when a saved person falls into sin, they have an adversary who is faithful to intercede for them.

On our Christian walk with God, we trip and fall sometimes. That is because of our flesh. Other times it's because the devil set traps, and we didn't see them. Before we were saved, we weren't tripped up. We just sinned because that's what we did. We weren't saved. Others should be able to see a visible change in our life. We have the Holy Spirit living inside of us to help us live a Holy life. When we do wrong, he convicts us so that we repent and turn from whatever wrong we have done. We may fall but we get up. We don't live in sin like we did before we came to know Christ. Now we run from sin not into it. Our actions will change if we have had a real encounter with God. A conversion which means to change from one form to another. Therefore, not staying the same. If you really want God and a relationship with him, you can have that. He will not come where He is not wanted. If you want Him, He will be there for you. As a matter of fact, the bible says in Revelation 3:20, "Behold I stand at the door and knock; and if any man hears my voice and opens the door. I will come in to him and will sup with him and he with me." Matthew 5:6 says, **"Blessed are those who hunger and thirst after righteousness for they shall be filled."**

Our actions change when we accept Christ and sell out for Him. We live a life totally different from our old life. Our life now has meaning and purpose. We know now that we have work to do. Many of us say we want a relationship with God. We don't want to part with the things of the world. Well, we can't have it both ways. We must choose who we will serve. I don't know if we understand or if we are just in love with the world. Maybe we think that god will just sweep our sins under the rug and forget about them. Only if we repent and forsake them. Make no mistake in Romans 6:23 it says, **"for the wages of sin is death, but the gift of God is eternal life in Christ Jesus our Lord."** Putting the things of this world before God is to make those things our god. That is idol worship and that's a sin against God. If you love the things of the world, you can't love God. In James 4:4 it says, **"ye adulterers and adulteresses know ye not that the friendship of the world is enmity with God. Whosoever therefore will be a friend of**

the world is an enemy of God."

Having the love of God in your heart is what makes the difference in our actions. We want to do better and change things in our lives that's not of God. Some things don't change overnight. The Holy Spirits works with us to change all things that's not of God. Before my encounter with the Lord, my focus was not on God at all. My main focus was looking good, dressing up, so that I could catch some man's attention. I went to church, but it was not to learn about God or give Him praise. Not to say that it wasn't helping me. It was. I would hear the word from time to time. Faith does come by hearing and hearing by the word of God. I'm sure some of the words seeped in among all the other motives I had for going to church. The same with the woman at the well, her focus seemed to be on men. That is until she met Jesus that day, and it changed her life forever as it did mine. I will never be the same and I have no regrets except that I didn't sellout to Christ sooner.

Her Life Changed

There is no way a person can come into contact with the almighty God and remain the same. This is what happened to the woman at the well. Her life changed. She went from being a woman of shame to a woman of reconciliation bringing others to the same truth that she had just been introduced to. Her words were, "Come see a man!" She wanted others to experience what she had. She knew that her life had changed, and it would be for the better and others could have that too. So, the next thing to do was to get the good news out to as many people as possible. She dropped her pot, which symbolizes everything holding her back from her new life. What's holding you back? What's keeping you from giving God your all? Some things from our past life need to be left there. We all know what our "thing" is. The thing that seems to always get you off track. Anything can be a stumbling block that could trip you up in the future, or get you sidetracked from your new path. The woman at the well had a new outlook on life. She now saw that her life didn't have to be the way it always was. Her life changed. She had new interests, new actions, a new life. This woman was of no social importance not to the people of the city. In fact, she has often been misused and often the very subject of gossip and jokes. Now she had met the Messiah. This event changed her life forever. She was so changed that even her appearance, behavior, and attitude changed. People listened eagerly to what she had to say. There is a radiance about anyone that has been in the presence of God. A freshness, a newness. In the book of 2 Corinthians 5:17 is says, **"Therefore if any many be in Christ, he is a new creature. Old things are passed away behold; all things are become new."**

This woman wasted no time finding someone to witness to and the people responded at least a good number of them did. They kept on coming to Him. It was her dynamic witness and the striking change seen in her that caused the enormous response. Her witness caused many to set out to find the Messiah for themselves. It's amazing how Christ can turn a life around. You can see people's lives miraculously transform right before your eyes. No one but God can bring about such a change. Don't ever think you are so bad that God cannot change you. God can make everyone brand new.

HERE IS SOME HELP

"After the rain is gone" is a metaphor I used for not being saved. So, there is no way you won't walk with God if it's still raining in your life. For better words, you have not accepted Jesus as your personal Lord and Savior. In the days of Noah, it had never rained before the flood. There was only a mist that came up from the ground to keep things from growing. Until that time the people had never seen it rain. I used rain to symbolize no covering, no protection from the weather or the evils of the world. This book would not be complete without some help on this journey of walking with God. This section is on how to keep your head above water. In John 16:3, it says, **"These things I have spoken unto you that in me ye might have peace. In the world ye shall have tribulation but be of good cheer; I have overcome the world."**

In other words, in the world we will have tribulation and distress and suffering. Be courageous, be confident, be filled with joy. Jesus has overcome the world. When faced with difficult situations how we make it through is with the Holy Ghost. God has given us His holy word. He has sent His Holy Spirit, which is our helper. He has taken down the petition that separated us from Him and made a way for us to come boldly to the throne of grace in our time of need. He has given us instruction to pray without ceasing. Everything we need is in the word of God. There is life in the word of God. I would like to share some of my personal experiences of help. How God alone came to my rescue in difficult times in my life.

The first real difficult time that I remember was when my father died. I was eight years old. I lost at that time the most caring person in my life. He was my daddy. That word and person carried a lot of weight with me. Being as young as I was, I didn't fully understand the impact that his death had on my life. I remember standing at the foot of his bed, as he folded his arms across his chest, closed his eyes and with one last deep breath, he was done. That memory is etched in my mind.

For some reason I didn't want anyone to see me cry. I didn't want anyone to see me cry. I went outside around the side of our house where no one could see me. There I cried alone. This was my first real loss that I can remember. My Daddy was the first man in my life to make me feel like I mattered. I was important to someone. One example was we all went to church with daddy on Sunday. We didn't have a car so we walked together with him and when church was over daddy would always buy us ice cream. We ate it on the walk home.

There was a lady that lived across the street from the church that sold treats for children. My father had this little black leather change purse that he would keep his change in and when he opened it up to pay for the ice cream, I saw he had more change left in it. So, the next day before I went to school I asked daddy for a nickel for chocolate milk. He told me he didn't have it. I left sad because I knew he had it. I had seen it when he opened his purse the day before. When I got home from school that day my daddy called me to him. I sat on his lap, and he told me, "Baby daddy is sorry for telling you that I didn't have a nickel, because that wasn't the truth. I had it, but daddy had something else he had to do with it. I should not have told you that I didn't have it. I am sorry that I didn't tell you the truth." That made me feel six feet tall. That my dad would apologize to me. That made me happy, and I will never forget that day.

Even then God was making a deposit into my life giving me something to hold on to in bad times. Even though my father is gone I still have that memory of the good he did. This is just one way we can cope with loss. Remember the good that a person brought into your life. On our walk with God, He will help us through the difficult times. He doesn't move all of our stumbling blocks, but he will lead us around them if we follow his lead.

Another time was the loss of my mother. Now my mother was quite different from my father. My father was kind and soft spoken, but my mother had a hard exterior, stern. I believe she was that way because she was left alone with my father gone so much out of town to work. My mother had eight boys and five girls to raise. I have been through hell and high waters to raise three children, so I can't imagine raising thirteen. That's the kind of God we serve. She made it. I would always hear her say, "I just pray to God to let me live to see all my children grown." When she died her baby was twenty-nine years old. Her prayer was answered. All of her children were grown. I thought I would die too when she died. God kept me just as when my father died.

During this time, I was a grown woman with children of my own. I understood death a little bit better, but still had a lot of growing to do in my relationship with God. Now without a mother or father, God was the only one I could turn to. He was there for me. This was the second heart wrenching loss in my life. Those were times when I thought I couldn't make it. Now that's not to say that there weren't other things that shook me to the core. I'm not trying to tell everything. I just want you to know that on our Christian walk with God every day is not going to be sunshine. Life will happen to everyone. It's how we handle it that matters. This big loss made me want a closer relationship with my creator. I had many hurts, pains, heartaches, broken in many places, and in some cases my soul was wounded. God brought me through them all. That is not to say that I will not have more. I will. But a good thing now is that I know God will be there for me. I've learned that even when we can't do it for ourselves, He carries us.

Another example, my closest daughter had a little boy at this time. He was about seven years old. He contracted a staph infection in his knee and leg. He was rushed to the hospital. He had been taken to the hospital two or three times before this and was treated and given antibiotics but didn't get any better. The last time was taken to the hospital he was rushed to another hospital and was seen by a specialist. They performed surgery on his leg and then his arm. They said they were washing out the infection. He was then placed on the strongest antibiotic that they had, but the staph infection was still spreading to other parts of his body. It got to a place where the doctors didn't know what to do. They described the infection as a dandelion flower. Those white puff balls when you blow on it the seed flies everywhere. This was what happened to my grandson. It spread to his lungs. He had blood clots and was put on blood thinners.

Of course, we all prayed and asked God to heal him. The doctors said there was nothing else they could do. I left the hospital and went home and into my prayer closet. I had to be alone, so I could talk to God and listen to what He had to say. We thought he would not make it. This time when I prayed, I heard in the spirit, "Pray God's will be done." I thought about it. I said to myself, but what if God's will be for him to leave us and go home to be with the Lord? As I struggled with this, I surrendered to Him and fell down on my knees and prayed, "God, whatever your will is I except that you know best." Shortly after my grandson started to get better.

Wow! What an awesome God we serve. There is nothing too small or large for God. Just take it to Him in faith. My faith was tested. I struggled and I passed. God is always with us on our daily walk with Him. The Bible says he Gives his angels charge over us to protect us and comfort us in times of need. The important thing is to not allow ourselves to get discouraged. Always stay close to God. Keep our lives in balance. Too much of anything is bad for us. Rest in God, in His love and work out your own soul's salvation with fear and trembling.

Daily walking with God can be so wonderful, and so hard at the same time. Whatever we have to face it's worth it. The joy of life here and eternal in the next.

SOME ADVICE FOR YOUR WALK

My sisters and brothers in Christ, my advice to you is to just KNOW. Know that the God of heaven is with you always. He will supply you with whatever you need. He will never leave us nor forsake us. He has promised that, so if we could just hide that in our hearts. When trouble and trials come up in our lives, we will know that he is there. God is working it out for your good. Here are a few scriptures that assure us of this.

John 16:33, **"These things I have spoken unto you, that in me ye might have peace. In the world ye shall have tribulation: but be of good cheer; I have overcome the world."**

Philippians 4:19, **"But my God shall supply all your need according to his riches in glory by Christ Jesus."**

Romans 8:28, **"And we know that all things work together for good to them that love God, to them who are the called according to his purpose."**

I wish I could tell you that when you except Jesus as LORD, all your troubles and problems go away. I love walking with God. I just love knowing that He is with me in my life. Whatever I may face, however hard it is, Jesus can't go wrong. In actuality when we except Jesus as LORD it's done. Our life is wrapped up and tied up in Him. Everything is complete. We must still go through the process of life. There are things in us that have to be worked out. This is just preparation ground here. We are getting ready for the LORD.

Philippians 2:12-13 reads, **"Wherefore, my beloved, as ye have always obeyed, not as in my presence only, but now much more in my absence, work out your own salvation with fear and trembling. For it is God which worketh in you both to will and to do of his good pleasure."**

There will be ups and downs, good times and bad. Jesus said it's finished. He has done the work. Now all believers are in the process of living a good life. We know how it ends. That's the best part. We put on the whole armor of God and get on with life.

Ephesians 6:11, **"Put on the whole armour of God, that ye may be able to stand against the wiles of the devil."**

FROM THE AUTHOR

My hope is that some of the questions that some had after reading my first book were answered in this second part. If not, we can have a sit-down and you can ask me personally. For those who wanted to know more about my rainy days, I started out talking about those things, but the Holy Spirit changed my direction. I had to follow His lead. He told me what to share. God is awesome and supreme in all His ways. He knows what's best for His children in this life. If we allow Him, He will keep us safe. Some things are not meant to be told. God is still working on all of us. This book is the second part of my first book, "Healing for Your Brokenness." That book stands alone with its information on a person's condition before finding God. This book gives a bit more information on my early personal life. Its information is on life with God, our daily walk with Him. At the same time, it's a continuation of the first book. They work great together.

The times in my life that I really didn't' know God were the times I called my rainy days. I had no covering, no savior, no protection. My understanding had not been opened. This book is, "After The Rain Is Gone" My life with God, having a covering, a savior, and someone to protect me always. My walk with God hasn't been an easy walk, because It's been a time of learning and getting to know God. How things work on this side. One thing I learned is that we have three enemies. They are the world, the devil, our own flesh. We struggle with the flesh. Our flesh always wants to do the opposite of what the Spirit wants for us.

All believers must crucify daily their flesh, in better words, put to death the flesh, in order to walk with God. Not to mention the enemy is always trying to bring God's people down. We must be willing to give up what we want for what God wants. We must give up our will for His will. Also, this world and all it has to offer. We must remember we don't belong to ourselves we've been bought for a price. That price was Jesus giving up His life on the cross so that we could live. We belong to God. We have the Holy Spirit living inside of us. It helps us. We don't have to do this alone. We have our helper. We must grow and learn how to allow the Holy Spirit to lead and guide us. We must learn how to follow His lead. Now the enemy will always make things seem worse than they are. Just remember no matter how hard things may seem, I can still say as David said in Psalm 84:10, **"For a day in thy courts is better than a thousand. I had rather be a doorkeeper in the house of my God, than to dwell in the tents of wickedness."**

www.ingramcontent.com/pod-product-compliance
Lightning Source LLC
Chambersburg PA
CBHW051557120626
46551CB00013B/1552